Marriage Is
a Promise of
Love

Blue Mountain Press ®

Boulder, Colorado

Marriage Is a Promise of Love

A collection of poems
Edited by Susan Polis Schutz

Library of Congress Catalog Card Number: 90-80732
ISBN: 0-88396-282-9

ACKNOWLEDGMENTS appear on page 62.

design on book cover is registered in U.S. Patent and Trademark Office.

Manufactured in the United States of America
First Printing: March, 1990

Blue Mountain Press ®

P.O. Box 4549, Boulder, Colorado 80306

CONTENTS

The Ten Secrets
of a Successful Marriage

— Having a wonderful partner.
— Communicating.
— Being intimately involved in one another's lives.
(Open, honest, touching, together. The closer you
are, the more secure you will feel.)
— Being happy as individuals. (And bringing good
things to the relationship from both directions.)

— Reaching out for dreams together.
— Always being there for one another. (Always.)
— Overlooking the few flaws. (But cherishing the
thousands of things that are so wonderful.)

— Remembering that rainbows follow rain.

— Always sharing. (Friends, families, dreams, desires.
Weaving together the fabric of your lives.)
— And always caring. (Always loving one another,
and being as happy and as giving and as thankful
as any two people could be.)

— Chris Gallatin

Marriage Joins Two People
in the Circle of Its Love

Marriage is a commitment to life —
to the best that two people can find and
bring out in each other. It offers
opportunities for sharing and growth no
other human relationship can equal, a
physical and emotional joining that is
promised for a lifetime.

Within the circle of its love,
marriage encompasses all of life's
most important relationships. A wife and
a husband are each other's best friend,
confidant, lover, teacher, listener, and
critic. There may come times when one
partner is heartbroken or ailing, and the
love of the other may resemble the tender
caring of a parent for a child.

Marriage deepens and enriches every facet of life. Happiness is fuller; memories are fresher; commitment is stronger; even anger is felt more strongly, and passes away more quickly.

Marriage understands and forgives the mistakes life is unable to avoid. It encourages and nurtures new life, new experiences, and new ways of expressing love through the seasons of life.

When two people pledge to love and care for each other in marriage, they create a spirit unique to themselves, which binds them closer than any spoken or written words. Marriage is a promise, a potential, made in the hearts of two people who love, which takes a lifetime to fulfill.

— Edmund O'Neill

Marriage Is a Wonderful Journey
That You Make Together

In marriage,
walk the path together,
side by side
whenever possible.
Remember to hold each other
when it is cold.
If the air becomes too close,
make a little space so each
   can breathe.
When the path is narrow,
pick one to go first.
Always be willing to follow;
don't be afraid to lead.
Trust your partner, trust yourself,
for marriage is a journey that
leads to great love.

— Mary E. Buddingh

Marriage Is a Lifetime of Love

Marriage embraces two people in love
  for a lifetime of sharing.
Marriage is a unique sharing
of day-to-day events.
It's having someone with you in spirit
to give support and love at all times.
Happiness in marriage doesn't just happen.
A good marriage requires time
  and devotion;
it's often filled with compromise
  and sacrifice,
as two people learn
to live together in harmony.

In marriage,
little things become big.
It's important to never take one another
  for granted
and to always be able to hold each other.
Marriage is having a mutual sense
of values and common objectives.
Being married means having
a lifetime best friend,
someone to laugh with, dream with,
  and cry with.
The true foundation of marriage
is giving love continuously
and unconditionally from one's heart.

—Sherry Jill Shaw-Levine

A marriage . . .
makes of two fractional lives
  a whole;
it gives to two purposeless lives
  a work,
and doubles the strength
of each to perform it;
it gives to two
questioning natures
a reason for living,
and something to live for;
it will give a new gladness
to the sunshine,
a new fragrance to the flowers,
a new beauty to the earth,
and a new mystery to life.

—Mark Twain

A Marriage Creed

Love is the strongest and
most fulfilling emotion possible
It lets you share
your goals, your desires, your experiences
It lets you share
your life with someone
It lets you be yourself
  with someone who will always support you
It lets you speak
your innermost feelings
  to someone who understands you
It lets you feel tenderness and warmth —
  a wholeness that avoids loneliness
Love lets you feel complete

But in order to have
a successful love relationship
you must make a strong commitment
  to each other and love
and you must do and feel everything
  within your mind and body
  to make this commitment work

You must be happy with yourself
  and you must understand yourself before
  you can expect someone else to be happy
  with you or to understand you
You must be honest about yourself
  and each other at all times
  and not hold any feelings back
You must accept each other the way you are
  and not try to change each other
You must be free to grow as individuals
  yet share your life as one
  but not live your life through each other
You must follow your own principles and morals
  and not follow what societal roles
  tell you to do

You must follow the philosophy that men and
   women are equal and not treat either person
   with inferiority in any way
You must be together always in your heart
   but not necessarily always in your activities
You must be proud of each other and love
   and not be ashamed to show
   your sensitive feelings
You must treat every day
   spent with each other as special
   and not take each other
   or your love for granted
You must spend time talking
   with each other every day
   and not be too busy with outside events
   that you are too tired for each other
You must understand each other's moods and
   feelings and not hurt each other intentionally
   but if your frustrations are taken out on each other
   you must both realize
   that it is not a personal attack
You must be passionate with each other often
   and not get into boring patterns
You must continue to have fun
   and excitement with each other
   and not be afraid to try new things
You must always work at love
   and your love relationship
   and not forget how important
   this relationship is
   or what you would feel like without it

Love is the strongest
and most fulfilling emotion possible
You will be living your dreams
   between awakenings
if you culminate your commitment to love
with marriage

                              —Susan Polis Schutz

On Marriage

Let there be spaces in your togetherness,
And let the winds of heaven dance between you.

Love one another, but make not a bond of love:
Let it rather be a moving sea between the shores of
  your souls.
Fill each other's cup but drink not from one cup.
Give one another of your bread but eat not from the
  same loaf.
Sing and dance together and be joyous, but let each
  one of you be alone,
Even as the strings of a lute are alone though they
  quiver with the same music.

Give your hearts, but not into each other's keeping.
For only the hand of Life can contain your hearts.
And stand together yet not too near together:
For the pillars of the temple stand apart,
And the oak tree and the cypress grow not in each
  other's shadow.

— Kahlil Gibran

In Marriage, Take the Time to Give Each Other More

Take the time to be gentle;
remember that words harshly spoken
trouble the spirit.
Take the time to talk to each other;
the secret to all understanding
is in open communication.
Don't be afraid to say
  what's on your mind,
and listen wisely.
Take the time to remember
that you chose one another
  to learn and to grow with;
you each have something valuable
to offer.
Be a good teacher
  and a good student.

Take the time to be alone,
so that you can gather your
   innermost thoughts
and share them with each other
   when you're together.
Take the time to be thankful.
You have chosen your path together;
take the time to make it
   the way you want it.
If change is needed,
do it gracefully.
Take the time to be loving;
it is the one thing everyone needs.
Always, in marriage,
take the time to give each other more.

—Gayle Saunders

The Heart of Marriage Is Memories

"The heart of marriage is memories;
and if the two of you happen to have
the same ones and can savor your reruns,
then your marriage is a gift of the gods."

—Bill Cosby

Ideals to Live by in Marriage

To fall in love over and over again...
   with the same person.
To be the best of friends.
To share the journey of life
   in the happiest way you can.
To be a woman; to be a man;
to bring the best
   each has to offer to the special
      union you two share.
To care enough to communicate
   openly and honestly.

To help one another along the way.
To say "I love you" — and have it
    convey the happiest single emotion
        any two people can
            ever say.

To be together today
    and to make the most beautiful
    memories you can to take with you
    into all of your tomorrows.

                              —Carey Martin

Marriage Celebrates
the Sharing of Two Unique Individuals

When you're married,
you join hands and become one.
As you walk
through life
together and not alone,
remember that you are
both unique and different
from each other.
Give your love openly and honestly.
Do not try to change each other;
your differences helped
bring you together.
Always respect and accept
what the other has to say,
even if you do not agree.
Remember that you are
two separate individuals.
You are one, you are partners,
you are living the same life,
yet your lives may be different.
You have yourselves and you have
  each other.
Take time to enjoy every day
you share together, and remember
that each day is a new beginning.

—Catherine Haukland

Love Can Always
See You Through the Difficult Times

Marriage is a union
of patience, caring,
 and devotion
that will take you through
 many changes,
that will call upon the strengths
and challenge the weaknesses
 of your relationship.
Yet as much as you love each other,
there will be times when you will
feel discouraged with each other.

It is important
  during these times
that you do not lose sight
of what made you form
  a union of marriage,
and that you each respect
  the other's right to be true
to their individual self.
It is important
to know deep in your heart
that giving and receiving
the freedom, compassion,
  and acceptance of love
are the greatest gifts two people
  can give each other.

—Wendy Choo

What Is a Marriage?

It is the most beautiful thing that
can happen between two people in love.

A marriage is more than just a husband
and a wife. It is a bridge which allows
the love of two very special people to
give meaning and worth and wonder to life.
It is a continual process of building; of
shaping; of communicating; and caring. It
is the deepest and sweetest understanding.
It is sharing todays and tomorrows together
and making each one more treasured and more
complete than anyone could make them alone.
A marriage is a home interwoven with hopes
and memories and dreams. The thankfulness
and love it can bring have no comparison.

Being happily married is the most
beautiful thing that can happen . . . to anyone.

—Collin McCarty

Marriage Is a Lifetime of Love

Marriage is the coming together
   of two very special people;
the uniting and bonding
   of two loves;
the commitment made by two people
   for a common purpose.
It is the blending
   of two people's ideas,
   feelings, habits, and desires.
It is taking
   the good with the bad;
   understanding the other's
   reasons and feelings.
But most of all, it is sharing,
   compassion, forgiving,
   and best of all,
      making up.

Marriage is the bonding
  of two unique people;
  the beginning of their legacy together;
  the start and strength
    of their family;
  the passion of their beliefs, actions,
    and values;
and the love that is given to their children
  and their children's children.

Marriage is what
  brings two people together,
while love is what
  keeps them together forever.

—Tim Roemmich

The Most Wonderful Commitment
in Life Is Being Married

In marriage
you make the most beautiful
commitment in life —
to love each other forever
You will share
work and play
happiness and sadness
goals and values
family and friends
excitement and boredom
You will build a life
which is stronger because
you are now part of a team —
a team which should go through life
holding hands
always cheering for each other
In marriage
you make the most beautiful
commitment in life —
two people
in love
joining together
to become
one forever

— Susan Polis Schutz

Marriage Is
a Celebration of Love

Being married is a beautiful feeling;
it makes whatever we do
seem wonderful and happy.
It gives us so many reasons
to smile,
or to tell the world
that someone is special to us —
someone who cares about us
the way we care about them.
Being married makes times of being together
go by so quickly
and times of being apart
seem to last forever.

Being married fills our lives with memories.
It is a unique feeling
that changes all the time,
but every different aspect
has a magic all its own.
The beauty of marriage is endless.
It is the essence of life
we all are longing to find,
longing to hold,
and dreaming of keeping forever
in our hearts.

—Deanna Beisser

Words to Live by
Within Marriage

To always be there for one another.
To help. To create. To live life fully.
To encourage. To share. To show that you
   care — even without the need for words.
To work for common goals. To simply enjoy.
To walk, hand in hand, along the paths
   that will take you to your dreams.
To make beautiful and lasting memories.
To have a relationship that is strong
   enough to weather any clouds that may
   come your way. To always communicate.
To fill your home with smiles and to have
   it be everything you want it to be.

To realize how wonderful it is that the
two of you are together . . . and to know
that the bond you share and the love
   that encircles you . . . will last forever.

— Collin McCarty

Marriage Fulfills the Dreams and Love Two People Share

Everyone searches
for one special person
they can share their lives with;
the other half who makes
  them whole,
like two notes blending together
to make a beautiful song,
or the colors that complement
each other to form a rainbow.
It is everyone's wish
to have a lifetime
  of sunny days,
a rainbow after every storm;
a lifetime of loving and living
and growing and giving,
of sharing and caring;
a lifetime of days together,
learning from the bad times
and cherishing the good times.

Marriage is everything your heart desires,
and the strength, courage, and
determination to work for it.
In marriage you take care of each other's heart
and hold on to what you share.
You hold it gently, so it doesn't smother,
and firmly, so it doesn't slip away.
Hold it so that it can grow,
and you can grow together,
and live and laugh and love together always.

—Glenda Willm

Marriage Is a Promise to Love

Marriage is a covenant
  between two people
who deeply sense that their lives are,
and always will be, shared as one.

Marriage is the fulfillment of a dream
and an awareness that reality also
can bring us the beauty of dreams.

Marriage is a promise that today
is the beginning of a future
that will nurture love, respect, honor,
and mutual faith as the greatest
strengths for its foundation.

Marriage is an understanding between
two sensitive, intelligent,
  and caring people
who have evidenced that true love
can survive all obstacles and grow
stronger with the passage of time.

— Edith Schaffer Lederberg

A Wife's Special Thoughts About Her Husband

A husband is the one special man who brings every happiness and shares every sweetness with the woman who is fortunate enough to be his wife. A husband is the one special soul who is the love of her life.

A husband is a desire to never be apart. He is the answer to one of the most important questions anyone can ask; he is whom you want to spend all of your days with . . . always. No one else is quite like him. No one else is capable of reaching you in the same way. There is something wonderful about him that brightens the days and makes dreams come true. He is the one man in the world you want to walk with along life's path. Together, the two of you have made such beautiful memories. Together, in the warmth of every today, you still do. And forever, he will be the one you want to be beside as you discover everything tomorrow has in store.

A husband is your one special man, and you wish he could really understand how wonderful he is.
   Because there is no one
         you could possibly love more.

—Laurel Atherton

A Husband's Loving Promise
to His Wife

Someone will always be here to love you.

Someone will always cherish
   the warmth of your smile and
   the happiness in your heart.
Someone wants to always be close enough
   to care in every way and to treasure
   each and every day spent together.

Someone will always keep you lovingly
      in mind,
   and will welcome every opportunity
      to find you in happy thoughts.

Someone will always know that life
   is good because of you, and that tomorrow
   has a bright and shining hope that
   wouldn't be there if you weren't here today.
Someone will always try to find the words
   to thank you for filling life with
   dreams come true and with beautiful
      memories.

Someone will always love you.

      . . . And that someone
         will always be your husband.

— Chris Gallatin

A Lasting Marriage
Is Based on Many Things

A close relationship is based
  on friendship.
A caring relationship is based
  on sharing and understanding.
A romantic relationship is based
  on giving freely and on the ability
  to receive gratefully and graciously.
An intimate relationship is based
  on openness and honesty.
An affectionate relationship is based
  on patience and acceptance.
A secure relationship is based
  not on promises, but rather
  on trust, respect, faithfulness,
  and the ability to forgive.
A lasting marriage is based
  on all of these, bound together
  by love.

— Michael C. Mack

Love Is the Most
Beautiful Feeling in Marriage

Love is
the strongest feeling known
an all-encompassing passion
an extreme strength
an overwhelming excitement

Love is
trying not to hurt the other person
trying not to change
   the other person
trying not to dominate
   the other person
trying not to deceive
   the other person

Love is
understanding each other
listening to each other
supporting each other
having fun with each other

Love is
not an excuse to stop growing
not an excuse to stop
  making yourself better
not an excuse to lessen one's goals
not an excuse to take the
  other person for granted

Love is
being completely honest
  with each other
finding dreams to share
working towards common goals
sharing responsibilities equally

Everyone in the world wants to love
Love is not a feeling
  to be taken lightly
Love is a feeling to be cherished
  nurtured and cared for
Love is
the reason for life

—Susan Polis Schutz

Marriage Means Being in Love
for the Rest of Your Life

Marriage is love
walking hand in hand together.
It's laughing with each other
about silly little things,
and learning to discuss big things
with care and tenderness.
In marriage,
love is trusting each other
when you're apart.
It's getting over disappointments
and hurts,
knowing that these are present
in all relationships.
It is the realization that
there is no one else in this world
that you'd rather be with
than the one you're married to.
It's thinking of new things
  to do together;
it's growing old together.
Marriage is being in love
for the rest of your life.

—Chris Ardis

When Two People Marry,
Their Lives Are Joined in Happiness

When two people marry,
they share equally with each other.
They become one.
A bond is built, along with trust
  and loyalty.
They accept each other for what they are.
They love each other for who they are.
They are there for each other
  to comfort when they are down.
When one hurts, the other hurts.
They communicate with each other.
The problems they have are worked out.
They work on their relationship together.
They learn to grow with each other.
They accept challenges as they come.

Sometimes they are scared,
   but they are always there for one another.
They are one,
but they have their own minds,
their own ideas, and different ways
   of thinking.
They love and learn, cry and feel.
They are there to help each other.
They are not perfect; they make mistakes.
Their lives are lived happily,
when two people marry.

—Tracey Kuharski-Miller

Marriage Is Two People
Sharing Everything in Life

In marriage
two people share
all their dreams and goals
their weaknesses and strengths
In marriage
two people share
all the joys and sadnesses of life
and all the supreme pleasures
In marriage
two people share
all of their emotions and feelings
all of their tears and laughter

Marriage is the most
fulfilling relationship
one can have
and the love that you share
as husband and wife
is beautifully forever

—Susan Polis Schutz

May Your Marriage Be Blessed
with a Lifetime of Happiness

Marriage is the joining
   of two people —
the union of two hearts.
It lives on the love
   you give each other
and never grows old,
but thrives on the joy
   of each new day. . .
Marriage is love.

May you always be blessed
   in your hearts
with the wonder of your marriage.

May you always be able to
    talk things over,
to confide,
to laugh with each other
and enjoy life together,
to share moments
of quiet peace
when the day is done.

May you be blessed
with a lifetime of happiness.

—Jill Ryynanen

Marriage Is the Greatest
Happiness of All

In a marriage, two people
become as one,
yet they are individuals,
each with their own ideas and goals.
In a marriage, two people
share their thoughts.
They give advice, sharing their feelings,
being open and loving.
They must trust each other
and hold on to faith
while going through ups and downs.
They have their smiles,
and they have their tears.
When one is low, it is up to the other
to support them, to get them
back on the right track.
Communication is the key.
Two people united learn so much.
They learn to depend
yet be independent,
sometimes letting each other
have time to themselves.
They care for each other and protect;
they make a family and become a lifeline.
They begin their dreams, their future,
loving and growing together.
With their commitment and true love,
they find happiness.

—Michele Gallagher

Love in Marriage Can Last Forever . . .

Love is something to share with a
  wonderful person;
    and once it's there, you've got to make
      it last.
Love isn't something to be
    taken for granted. It's something
    to be nurtured and cared for and
      caressed.
Love can last forever. . . if you want
    it to.
Love isn't tough and tentative;
    it's wonderful and gentle and tender.
Love is mysterious, but it asks that
    you share no secrets. Love is blind, but
    it asks that you see how happy it can
      make you.

Love is more like a flower than a tree;
   the wrong things can hurt it so easily.
   But the right things can make it more
   beautiful and more fragrant than
   anything else your life has
      ever known.

Love is something to be treated as the
   best of all blessings; and as your own
   little miracle
      that will keep coming true
      as long as you want it to.

— Barin Taylor

ACKNOWLEDGMENTS

We gratefully acknowledge the permission granted by the following authors, publishers, and authors' representatives to reprint poems or excerpts from their publications.

Mary E. Buddingh for "Marriage Is a Wonderful Journey. . . ." Copyright © Mary E. Buddingh, 1990. All rights reserved. Reprinted by permission.

Sherry Jill Shaw-Levine for "Marriage Is a Lifetime of Love." Copyright © Sherry Jill Shaw-Levine, 1990. All rights reserved. Reprinted by permission.

The Mark Twain Foundation for "A marriage," by Mark Twain. From the book THE LOVE LETTERS OF MARK TWAIN, edited by Dixon Wecter. Copyright © 1947, 1949, by The Mark Twain Foundation. All rights reserved. Reprinted by permission.

Alfred A. Knopf, Inc., for "On Marriage," by Kahlil Gibran. From the book THE PROPHET. Copyright © 1923 by Kahlil Gibran; renewal Copyright 1951 by Administrators C.T.A. of Kahlil Gibran Estate, and Mary G. Gibran. All rights reserved. Reprinted by permission of Alfred A. Knopf, Inc.

Gayle Saunders for "In Marriage, Take the Time to Give Each Other More." Copyright © Gayle Saunders, 1990. All rights reserved. Reprinted by permission.

Doubleday for "The Heart of Marriage Is Memories," by Bill Cosby. Excerpt from the book LOVE & MARRIAGE by Bill Cosby. Copyright © 1989 by Bill Cosby. Used by permission of Doubleday, a division of Bantam, Doubleday, Dell Publishing Group, Inc.

Catherine Haukland for "Marriage Celebrates the Sharing. . . ." Copyright © Catherine Haukland, 1990. All rights reserved. Reprinted by permission.

Wendy Choo for "Love Can Always See You Through. . . ." Copyright © Wendy Choo, 1990. All rights reserved. Reprinted by permission.

Deanna Beisser for "Marriage Is a Celebration of Love." Copyright © Deanna Beisser, 1990. All rights reserved. Reprinted by permission.

Glenda Willm for "Marriage Fulfills the Dreams and Love. . . ." Copyright © Glenda Willm, 1990. All rights reserved. Reprinted by permission.

Edith Schaffer Lederberg for "Marriage Is a Promise to Love." Copyright © Edith Schaffer Lederberg, 1990. All rights reserved. Reprinted by permission.

Michael C. Mack for "A Lasting Marriage Is Based on Many Things." Copyright © Michael C. Mack, 1990. All rights reserved. Reprinted by permission.

Tim Roemmich for "Marriage Is a Lifetime of Love." Copyright © Tim Roemmich, 1990. All rights reserved. Reprinted by permission.

This book is printed on fine quality, laid embossed, 80 lb. paper. This paper has been specially produced to be acid free (neutral pH) and contains no groundwood or unbleached pulp. It conforms with all of the requirements of the American National Standards Institute, Inc., so as to ensure that this book will last and be enjoyed by future generations.